Misplaced Love

To

Fortified Faith

Written by: Jessica Zarling

Misplaced Love to Fortified Faith

ISBN: 979-8-9989203-4-9

Chapters

To Fortified Faith

Dear Reader,

"But now, after that ye have known God, or rather are known of God, how turn ye again to the weak and beggarly elements, whereunto ye desire to be in bondage again."(Galatians 4:9 KJV)

This book is describing exactly how my fleshly desires (which stemmed from perceived[1] voids) led me back to momentary bondage again; how willful sin brought forth death due to these idols erected from the broken places of my past. This is a story of three men and myself over the course of over 20 years. All the while God was whispering to me, and I was ignoring His critical promptings.

The first man was the best option. We were both young and still pure regarding physical intimacy. While neither of us had a particularly close walk with Jesus at the time, he and I both would at a later time. Unfortunately, at the age of seventeen, I had already disqualified myself from a good

---

[1] Websters Dictionary definition of perceived. 1) regarded in a specified way -used to say how something or someone is seen or thought of. 2.) recognized through the senses.

man due to unaddressed wounds and lack of both external and internal validation.

The second man who would become my husband and I came from very familiar and toxic backgrounds. Upon reflection, it was no wonder I felt right at home with him. Although I knew Jesus Christ as my Savior, had yet to make Him Lord of my every moment and recognize Him as my first Husband. Instead, I was looking to this unsaved man to be who I needed rather than recognizing my First Love had already given me His all on the cross on Calvary. The third man was another worldly man who had so many loving qualities—honesty being number one. His gentle and understanding nature made it all the harder to accept the reality the enemy was successfully using us both in ways that were not pleasing to God.

This book is also my love letter to you. Although it is possible to return to former ways after giving your life to Christ, the unwavering faith in His truth can enable you to choose God's best, in contrast to that which attempts to momentarily satisfy, which only leads to death. The death of your relationship with Christ, death of the peace He promises, and death to the purpose and plan He has for your future is something you can avoid. Too often we make excuses for our sin when His way can help us avoid these painful traps. He promises in His Word that with every temptation He has made a way of escape. My hope for you in writing this book is you not only see the way of escape but take it.

In sharing the mistakes I made and the valuable lessons learned, may this book convey the importance of fortifying your heart and mind in truth. Rather than following down the path of misplaced love, even if it is the only thing you have ever known, you can claim every promise in His word as your own, walking out the inheritance He died for you to have: *"abundant life in Christ"* (paraphrased John 10:10 KJV).

As we walk through this life, there are certain points when we realize what we had formerly believed was simply not true. This is because so many of our beliefs are formulated according to the world system and, speaking for myself, come from movies, songs, and tv where true romance seemed to exist. This love where individual happiness and feeling good is the goal is contrary to the unconditional love that can only be obtained with the help of the Holy Spirit through continual forgiveness and love towards one another found in Christ.

My prayer is for your heart to grasp His love, for your mind to be renewed according to His truth which is found in His Word, that your soul be healed, and even in its former brokenness, your faith would now override every temptation the enemy uses to lure you off the Rock, that is in Christ, back into the past, also known as sinking sand. You do not have to go back to Egypt, returning to what may be the only thing you have ever known. You can forge new pathways with the Great Shepherd in your heart and mind, altering your beliefs and subsequently changing your life.

We are living in a real battle ensuing all around us, which can also impact us internally. My hope is you will not become a casualty of living for less than every promise in His Word being a yes and amen. I pray that you and I will not forfeit our inheritance by being disobedient to the Word of God. He is a good father and every gift He gives is perfect.

The enemy is looking for the areas in your life not fortified in the Word of God by faith. It is not enough to just know the Word; you must believe it and stand firm when the enemy comes in like a flood. Planting the Word deep in the heart is something you and I must be diligent in pursuing and may look slightly different for each person. However, I encourage you to do whatever it takes to get the Word in and to protect it. As the Word says, we are to be faithful in *"guarding your heart above all else, for out of it flow the issues of life"* (Psalm 4:23 KJV). As we are obedient in the process, you and I will see the beautiful kingdom unfold day by day!

This book is written as a means of a seed dying. My pride, flesh, and the appearance of having it all together has to die. I am inviting the Lord and you into this area of brokenness, trusting fully for His healing, not just for me, but for you also. I am so thankful for His promise to give us *"double for our shame"* (paraphrased Isaiah 61:7).

We all have been sold similar lies and bought them as though they were just the wages of living life. Yet God promises us abundant life in Christ, the one who bore our sins, so we could be free and walk each day in victory. By shining a light on the areas of darkness with the truth of God's Word, you will be able to replace old faulty habits with the truth and light of His love. Unfortunately, by not doing this, I found myself repeating old patterns only to be even more convinced that these old patterns lead to death. Now I am even more confident His way is life. Once the truth of His Word is continually being applied in our heart and mind, it can be the light that illuminates the pathway out of bondage and out of darkness into His marvelous light.

Introduction to Misplaced Love

Often times our behaviors clearly indicate what we believe about God. Our behaviors reveal what obstacles remain in our heart, what needs to be removed, uprooted, and/or surrendered in order to allow His pure love to flow through. What are some of the areas getting in the way of seeing His relentless and steadfast love? When we are able to rest in His love, by faith, no matter what this life brings, we are reflecting His true, mature love. May we all faithfully declare Philippians 1:6, "He who hath begun a work in us will bring it to completion in the day of Christ Jesus."

When something is misplaced, it is out of its proper and authoritative place. Love, who is God, is the ultimate authority, being our Creator and therefore needs to remain in first place in order for His predestined plan to succeed!

My trusted prayer is He will show us and redirect us in prioritizing Him. He will faithfully help us identify the patterns necessary to experience newness of life.

In my season of looking back to the past, experiencing grief and loss, I began operating out of "perceived" voids. In reality Christ had already filled these areas of my life. It just wasn't in the ways I originally expected or envisioned. Thankfully, He shone His loving light into the darkened areas of my heart and mind, and He so graciously, with the power of the Holy Spirit, highlighted those areas with the truth of His Word.

This book is the journey God took me on. I am trusting Him to take you on a similar journey of healing, deliverance, and greater freedom as you reclaim your identity in Him.

Misplaced Love

Journey Out of Egypt
into the Promised Land

The Lord often reminds me, "You didn't know you were blind until you could see," to encourage me when I am speaking with those who don't yet realize their need of the Lord and Savior Jesus Christ. Can I tell you I also realize,

"Working out my own salvation with fear and trembling (Philippians 2:12 KJV)" is quite the daily task, especially during challenging times. When we get saved (born again) we begin to see things differently, like a fog slowly lifting. This is the process of consecration, or where His reshaping of our lives begins, and the external idols begin to fall away.

Then the time comes to realize there are internal idols that have been erected within our hearts and our minds. These idols need excavation. This process is additionally painful because these idols seem to be rooted in the very fiber of your flesh being and often it is because they have been modeled and passed down through the generations. Yet, we must remember He promises us that *"in Him we are new creations"* (2 Corinthian 5:17 KJV).

Are you ready to go on this journey together of trusting Him with all of our hearts?

I am so grateful for the greater freedoms and victory in Jesus Christ our Lord. I want to bring to remembrance the fact that together, you and I can journey out of the Egyptian mindset of slavery and move towards greater freedoms according to His Word.

Recognizing Patterns

In my younger years, I believed that in a new environment, things would be different. This belief also made me somewhat of a runner. This was one of the reasons I joined the military, being willing to embark on a new yet unfamiliar adventure. When I was far away from everyone I had loved and everything was new, I ended up still somehow clinging to the old, even though I had every intention not to. The old and familiar I had been so anxious and excited to leave behind was closely following waiting for the opportunity to enter back in.

Often times we think what needs to change is external, like if I was able to live here or there, or have access to this or that, then things will be better. Through my own life and upon reflection, the Lord has highlighted to me in times past how He has blessed me by setting up opportunities to escape from Egypt. Almost immediately, however, I have opened the door to allow Egypt back in. This is because Egypt was familiar, comfortable, and basically all I had known. What I really needed was to step out of my comfort zone.

In times of transition, there seemed to be a greater level of emotional vulnerability, desperately needing to find roots in new soil. By allowing Egypt[2] back in, my forward momentum was derailed. Although a man living for the kingdom of God has been my true "born again" heart's desire for the last nine years, I rather found myself yet again with another man similar to those I have known for the majority.

These unsaved men, from my past, are ones who remind me of my unsaved parent and my earliest worldly programming where my beliefs about relationships were formed in my subconscious. Watching the people I loved and expected to be loved by but rather they were choosing a life of sin, idolizing things that could never fulfill (substances, relationships, and connecting themselves intimately to those they were not married too). These men stir up the same hope

---

[2] please note that the specific Egypt this book refers to was a man, and at that time not a God-fearing man, one bound up by the world similar to the behaviors my parents modeled in my growing up years.

I had for my parents growing up. Waiting, longing and hoping they would have an encounter with God that changes everything for the better. Even as a child it was clear my parents were missing something. Now as a follower of Christ, surrendered to the Holy Spirit, I know what was missing was salvation and a personal relationship with Him. My initial hope with each past worldly man was to shine the light and love of God's truth upon them. Rather the result ends up being entangles in a web of toxic emotions, lies (I begin telling myself) and worst of all, fornication.

I say worst because the Bible says explicitly, *"flee fornication"* (1 Corinthians 6:18 KJV) as in do not physically go near any temptation, but rather turn in the opposite direction and get as far away as quickly as possible. *"Fornication is not the will of God."* Also, the Bible emphasizes that *"fornication is a sin against one's own body."* Do you need any more reasons as to why fornication is not pleasing to God? I certainly do not; unfortunately, it took a few more serious pitfalls for me to really get these truths deeply ingrained in my brain.

Saints, I must remind you every time we step off the Rock, that is Christ who is also the eternal Word, we will be on sinking sand and deeper and deeper will you go. Shame will attempt to silence you, and until you cry out for help from the Lord and others, the further you can potentially sink back into sin. Can I tell you sinking sand will kill you if you don't allow someone to pull you out? God's arm is not short and he can reach you anytime and in any place, no matter how deep you have sunk. God is so faithful to redeem and restore and to place our feet back upon the only sure foundation we have: Jesus Christ.

"I will lift mine eyes to the hills, from whence cometh my help. My Help comes from the Lord, the maker of heaven and earth" (Psalms 121:1-2 KJV).

I also want to share that in my own journey, being transparent about my struggle allowed others to pray and intercede for me as well. This was after I recognized a pattern and then contemplated why the Lord says, *"I give more grace to the humble"* (James 4:6 KJV). Incorrectly, I bought the lie of thinking I needed to do this walk with Christ alone and ultimately it was another area where my beliefs and mind needed to be further transformed. He didn't refer to us as a body of Christ for us to stand or, worse, sink alone.

My missteps and regression began when previous traumatic loss and grief had been stirred up by observing similar past cycles of previous ignorance (darkness) to God's Word in a close relative. It was a time where I was completely against taking any elders advice, thinking I knew what was best for my life and being reminded of all the negative consequences which stemmed from that. Consequences that not only affected me but my children as well. This observation shifted my focus back to the past rather than being present and/or looking towards the future.

God's Word declares, *"But this one thing I do, forgetting those things which are behind and reaching forth unto the things which are before. I press towards the mark for the prize of the high calling of God in Christ Jesus* (Philippians 3:13-14 KJV). In hindsight it is clear, staying present with faith-filled declarations was what was needed, along with continual prayer for my family members and myself not to fall into any bondage.

FAITH FILLED DECLARATION

Father God, in the name of Jesus, by the power of the Holy Spirit,

I am trusting after falling back into these sinful patterns that You have now fortified these areas with the truth of Your Word according to Your Great love. I am trusting by faith that every person who reads this book will be able to apply Your Word of truth, that no lie or perceived void from the enemy will continue to prevail against them! I am trusting fully that You will *"order our steps in Your Word"* (Psalm 119:133) and to victory. I pray that they will not only live fully and freely according to Your Word, but You would equip them to teach others to do the very same. We thank You, Jesus, for being the Way, our escape, and that we stand in victory declaring Your perfect love has already won!

Amen

Upon reflection, the awareness of generational cycles and patterns of family sin were coming to the forefront of my mind as my niece was about to be delivered from the womb into this earth. My sister and I are sixteen years apart, so in many ways I feel more like a mother to her. At this time, her new marriage reminded me of every ungodly reason for my own marriage twenty years prior. The mindset I had at the time was darkened to the reality that the true purpose of marriage is an honorable covenant and union whose sole purpose is to glorify God. It is a loving covenant with a kingdom purpose, which even extends outside of the home.

In addition to recognizing the numerous generational curses (addiction, fornication, sexual immorality, domestic abuse) which had run rampant in my family on both sides and all their negative implications, I began to experience a series of personal losses. By the time I began a relationship with this familiar guy, four people had already passed away who reminded me of various seasons in my life. It was as if I was drowning in grief, because not only was I grieving people who had died but also people who were still alive, being absent also due to generational bondage.

This season of regression can best be described as a dance with familiar spirits. The loss of these people, especially a young sister in Christ who I assumed to have a lifetime with, crushed me. She was a very close friend and dear sister who was just learning what it meant to be loved by Christ. In this time of grief, my dreams for the future seemed to have been washed away in the shock and bewilderment which was compounded by loss after loss, occurring month after month, in a short period of time. My emotional process could not keep up and it was as though a fog came over me.

My prayer for you is as the Bible says to be *"wise as a serpent and gentle as a dove"* as you seek His wisdom in the areas you need fortification of faith in. May it would be clear what areas the enemy has been tripping you up, the areas your flesh gets into agreement with the devil and you boldly declare with the help and aid of the Holy Spirit, "No more!" For the Word of God declares, *"You are more than a conqueror,"* (paraphrased Romans 8:37) and so this is our promise, and we will protect it and keep it planted deep within our hearts, trusting every time temptation comes, this truth will spring forth as His Word becomes fulfilled in us.

Temptations

First, I want to say the enemy knows the particular desires that will tempt your flesh. He definitely knew mine, and he knows how to use the good that God has planted inside of me to lure me outside the protective bounds of God's design. The enemy always has a bait and a twist to try and hook us back into sin. In this instance, the man I was involved with made it clear up front he didn't want me judging him or excluding him from my dating options because of his lifestyle. How could I judge him when my own past included the same behaviors that he was engaged in? I was very familiar with his lifestyle... too familiar.

The greatest mistake I made was not accepting and embracing that it was necessary to have additional protective measures in place, especially in this time of greater vulnerability. I needed to seriously protect my walk with Christ and not feel bad even if he chose to view my boundaries as judgmental. If he thought I was judging by saying I did not want to date a man who smoked, drank, and went out, I needed to radically stand on my protective boundaries and move on. Yet there was this pull because it was all so familiar, and I convinced myself it was important for him to know I cared for him at a deeper level beyond his current behaviors and choices. That thinking was a part of the slippery slope which led me back into the mire of sin.

God gave me a word years ago while going through recovery from alcohol and drugs. It was a time of great revelation and pruning away. It was a time of acknowledging the past, grieving and letting go to embrace the new. He spoke a quiet but firm prompting to my heart, "We are either bound by the love of Christ or bound by lesser things."

Years after God's revelation, I repeated a sinful pattern which left me emotionally bound. In contrast, God made it known to me that His binding is meant to be a protective layer around us, a cocoon so to speak. This protection intends that no man except for our God-ordained husband may lovingly and tenderly unwrap on her wedding night. This man is one who is committed to learning about Christ, walking in His ways, and loving us the way He intends.

God has made you as a precious gift to only be shared with your husband, and this sacred union has been swallowed up in the vile filth of the world culture we are currently experiencing. However, we as kingdom people can learn to tell the truth and shame the devil by demonstrating how we have learned that God's plan is best. His plan entails certain requirements to protect us, our children, and the generations to come.

Besides our own fleshly desires, the devil, who is also the father of lies, plays a role in our sin when we choose to disobey God's will and perfect plan. Looking back, I have identified that there are a series of events that happened before I chose to fornicate. These could be a combination of ungodly fleshly thoughts followed by ungodly fleshly responses. What I want to highlight are the areas that became stumbling blocks. These were internal areas in my heart and mind still in need of renewal, needing the foundational belief that His Word was, is, and will always be more foundational than any emotional storm I could ever experience.

Fleshly Desires

"Flee also youthful lusts; but follow righteousness, faith, charity, peace, with them that call on the Lord with a pure heart" (2 Timothy 2:22 KJV).

While experiencing a lot of emotional pain and sadness, it is natural to look for relief, to desire some laughter, some light heartedness, and something opposite of the current reality. What woman doesn't want to be desired, to be protected, to believe there is a man who has her back? A strong shoulder to lean on? What started with physical proximity, being present, laughing and watching movies, turned into sending pics in my fitted clothing. Not just a regular pic though... a filtered one where you look like a model even though you don't have a drop of makeup on. Then came the heart eye emojis and all the favorable responses which brought a smile to my face and made me feel desired, which temporarily soothed and distracted me from the hurt, grief, and pain. These texted pictures led to more and became a major part of the ongoing sin pattern.

I justified that this texting was more than just being desired in a shallow surface level way. My thought process justified my involvement. If it was a random person I didn't know, an attraction based on mere appearance would be offensive to me. To be known for my character and personality has always mattered more than simply being found attractive. In some regard, I convinced myself he knew me since we were around each other when we were younger, and he heard about my life through the years. What I especially appreciated about him was he made no attempt to flirt. He was unlike other guys in this regard which made him more attractive.

As I began identifying the patterns that were drawing him and me back into sin, I had to delete the filter photo app from my phone. Then I needed to take into account the time which I was most prone to take and text pictures. Once this day and time was apparent, I had to make other plans. Even more than that, I had to play the tape to the end to know where these actions would lead was not the desired end that would honor God (relationship, marriage, family, etc.). In an honest assessment, he and I were not in any place or position at this time to get where the Lord would ask us to be in order to be wed. The longer I continued to succumb to momentary desires, the true heart desires pertaining to the kingdom were on hold—or worse, being delayed or overrode. In every decision, there seem to be two options, choices and justification that appeal to the flesh or choices that pertain to the kingdom of God.

Battle plan

Identify the youthful lusts in your life…

What time are you most likely to begin thinking on these lusts?

What is at the root of this desire?

How can you crucify this root and invite God in to plant something pure and lovely?

What is an alternative course of action?

Who are those you know who are living by faith and can keep you accountable in purifying your heart? If you do not know any yet, where could you meet some?

Affection and Closeness

"Can a man take fire into his bosom and his clothes not be burned?" (Proverbs 27:1 KJV).

One of the most recent losses I experienced during this time was my aunt. At my aunt's funeral I felt so vulnerable. Not just because my aunt had died, but also because my mom wasn't there and has been missing in action for the last fifteen years. She was now the only person alive in the preceding generation remaining in our family. It was also difficult being around my family as they still had not known Jesus or the concept of His great personal sacrifice for the forgiveness of sins. It was a struggle to witness how they were condemning my mom for actions stemming from her addiction, while still having their own battles.

Another young friend of mine had died just six weeks before my aunt's funeral, leaving her baby girl behind. This was after two other friends (one from the past and one current brother in Christ) had taken their own lives. These losses were all in a succession of four months. My heart was in a place of trying to understand what God was doing in the midst of all these shattered families left behind. I simply wanted to be held, to be seen, to have someone tell me it was going to be ok. These longings brought me back to a childhood where those simple assurances were just not there.

This season of loss and desolation deep in my subconscious left me with the sense that there was a void to be filled. In reality, there was darkness, a momentary ignorance of the goodness of God. It was up to me to shine the light of God's truth, His Word, into these areas and to enlist others to help as well. However, I was too busy trying to understand the circumstances, to make sense of things far beyond my comprehension. Rather I needed to remember "...*His ways are higher as are His thoughts* (Isaiah 55:8 KJV)." To "*trust in the Lord with all thine heart; and lean not unto my own understanding*" (Proverbs 3:5 KJV).

These perceived voids created just the right environment for the enemy to be knocking at the door. At my aunt's funeral service, one of my cousin's old best friends and I started talking and laughing, attempting to cover the sadness of the day with some lightheartedness. He offered to give me a ride home, but my dad was coming to get me, so I turned down that offer. Here was where the emotional pull towards backsliding began.

As the snow began to fall on my drive home, I texted my cousin to get his friend's number to thank him for the offer to drive me home. After texting him my appreciation, he wanted to stop by. I convinced myself having company seemed necessary in this time of grief. We would have some laughs, reminisce, and without all the additional negativity. It would be completely harmless.

In hindsight, I should not have gotten his number or text and should have just lifted a prayer up of thanksgiving for Him (the Lord) getting me home, but rather I continued to operate from a place of a perceived void where emotions were clouding my vision. I was longing for connection in this ongoing season of grief opening my door wide, all the while telling myself the reasons why he and I were not a good match, believing this moment to be an exception to the rule of the temptation that can occur being alone with someone of the opposite sex. Anytime we believe we are an exception to the rule, most likely there is a root of pride coupled with a lie.

Within ten days of his visit to my home, and due to a false sense of comfort with this man whom I had been around in my early adult life, a baby was conceived the first time we had sex together. Even as I write this I am still shocked about the whole matter. Can I also say as soon as I opened the door to him, my thoughts began to be focused on him instead of the thoughts and plans God had for me in His righteous will? Worries for him began to consume me regarding his lifestyle. I recognized that he was surrounded by dangers far greater than when I had lived in the same environment. The worries were also because of the shared sin we kept returning back to, even though I had every intention not to after each occurrence.

It was so reminiscent of being a little girl worried for my mom when she went out and was getting intoxicated, wondering if she would make it home safely. However, this was now the dad to my unborn child. Clearly, I had strayed from the righteous path and momentarily lost kingdom focus. It was almost as if a spiritual amnesia came over me and I was now in a new way reliving a cycle I had fought so hard with the Lord Jesus to escape.

Consequences of Sin

I felt such a weight of disappointment, having a baby with an unsaved man who wasn't in a position to marry me. Also, knowing our baby would be between two homes was similar to my own painful childhood. Remember, the Bible says, *"Do not be unequally yoked, for what fellowship does light have with darkness?"* (2 Corinthians 2:14 KJV).

I desperately needed to keep myself at peace, to be loving and forgiving in the midst of everything contrary to what I knew God really wanted for me.

After the first trimester, at seventeen weeks, I went in for a prenatal checkup. They put on the monitor to hear the heartbeat and there was only silence. The nurse pulled up the baby on the ultrasound and there was just an image of a still little ghost, which no longer had a rapidly beating heart. This was the baby I envisioned would be a living child outside of my womb. Also having imagined him as a toddler, I realized all of this was not to be. I was even more heartbroken having just recently gotten to a hopeful place of raising our baby in the Lord. I was finally feeling stronger physically, emotionally and spiritually in the Lord and understanding a greater depth of his forgiveness in spite of my flesh, "that children are a blessing of the Lord," in spite of how they were conceived. It wasn't until later I realized this also applied to me having been born in the same manner, between two people who were not well suited for each other. The weight of the generational cycles had now not only been witnessed but personally experienced as well.

I immediately texted the guy, letting him know our baby died. I figured we would now be able to go our separate ways, yet he also was just coming to terms with the reality of us having a baby. He asked to come over. Although I just wanted the whole situation to be behind us, I was once again unable to set the boundary as the tsunami of grief washed over me. He kept calling while I was absorbing the shock of it. He came over immediately, shortly after I arrived home from the hospital. We lay down side-by-side, and he wiped the flood of tears from my eyes as I cried and cried. This moment of tenderness and his presence at this moment would come to mean a lot to me. The significance meant more than any singular moment should because of the previous absence of this tender attentiveness.

Losing a baby is a tragedy! Losing a baby while not in a secure relationship only adds to the pain. He was not going to remain by my side as we weren't even in a relationship. This was one of the hardest things I had ever experienced. I longed for the baby to be alive. I longed for this man, who I momentarily had a future tie with to remain by my side. Never had I ever felt so alone in my life. So few people knew of the baby, but once I opened up about it, others shared their losses which occurred in the womb as well. I realized as the stories were shared that preterm loss is another heartbreaking situation so many do not talk about. It took me another year to grieve the situation with him and the baby. This was one of the most painful times in my life because all along I knew it was wrong but went ahead anyhow, letting my grief and fleshly needs based on perceived voids override the perfect will of God for my life.

Thankfully, I knew I was forgiven, yet the consequences of being forever changed in this tragic loss remained. This was where things began to shift, and I realized what was needed; fortified faith.

"In the way of righteousness is life, and in the pathway thereof there is no death" (Proverbs 12:28 KJV).

Dear Ladies and Gentlemen,

While I know it is not everyone's desire to be married, please examine your heart and know if you do have the desire to marry, you are never wrong to wait for the one who wants the very same. Whether like me, you come from a broken home built on fornication, or a family where divorce runs rampant, please allow the *desires of your heart come to pass as you delight yourself in the Lord* (paraphrased Psalm 37:4 KJV).

If you do not want to be married or committed and it is because of past grief, hurt, or pain, please talk and process it with a trusted person, whether it be church family or a professional. Your experiences, emotions, grief, loss, and unmet needs all matter immensely to God. These are not things meant to be carried, but to be poured out so His perfect love can flow in. We only have this one life, and our choices truly set an example for the generation to follow. Please allow His very best to be your lead and your guide. Our babies deserve to have both a mom and a dad present, providing the feeling of being safe and secure as they grow, with parents continually being led by the Holy Spirit.

This best can only happen after you release your own hurts, pains, and unmet expectations first. The lusts of the flesh that are not pleasing to God must be recognized and combated. Don't believe the lies of the enemy that you have to do this life alone. This seems to be particularly prevalent in American culture. Even if you already have kids, He is a faithful provider but first you must believe you are worthy to receive His abundant provision outlined in His Word. Even if you struggle with worthiness, His love reaches, transforms. and changes you when you are willing to begin seeing things His way. The good news is as you receive His promises, you can model living this new life and pass these realities down to your children and grandchildren, shifting the generations to come.

Taking an Honest Assessment

"Examine yourselves, to see whether you are in the faith. Test yourselves. Or do you not realize this about yourselves, that Jesus Christ is in you? – unless indeed you fail to meet the test"(2 Corinthians 13:5 ESV).

Upon reflection, the following areas and thought processes caused me to remain stuck in old patterns and responses. These sticking points included longing for connection in the loss of our baby, still looking for a man to lead in doing what was right, and the early correlation I had between pity and love. This was a combination of fleshly desires, which needed a greater understanding of how to practically apply the Word, how to wait on His perfect timing, and trusting Him to help me form new healthier patterns of relational operating.

It was also clear to me that while I had large amounts of faith in certain areas, there was a rocky soil in my heart when it came to relationships. I needed that debris to be cleared out so that seeds of truth could go deeply in the good soil of my heart by faith in His love. To allow His truth to take root in me deeply, I had to get out of the way. By "I," I am referring to my flesh.

The initial longing I had for connection remained after our baby passed. The loss of the baby impacted both of us. We both had begun our journey in a season of grief, as he had also recently lost a friend in a tragic way. I would go back and forth in my mind, over and over again, wanting to tell him my experience with the grief and loss. At times when I would, he would be very understanding, as he had lost a baby at twenty weeks twenty years prior.

As the day-to-day emotional waves of grief continued, I discovered that there would be other times when it would not be a good time for me to text him. When he would try to place a boundary between us and tell me to write in my journal instead of bombarding him with my emotional weight, after many reminders, I was able to finally do so.

My ultimate desire was to grieve this loss and heal together, however that wasn't possible either. As far as I could see, due to our different lifestyles, there was no future for him and I. There was a tremendous feeling of being caught between a rock and a hard place. While the severing was painful, it was necessary, and I am thankful for that process and being able to share my journey with you with God's help. It requires identifying the exact thoughts that were keeping me stuck in a cycle that was no longer healthy for either one of us. Once these thoughts were identified, then applying new biblical thoughts from the foundation of a renewed mind would ultimately help me be obedient.

Still Desiring for a Man to Lead

My time in this ungodly soul tie extended for much longer than needed from my perspective, because I still wanted him to lead in doing what was right which would have required him to end communication. I tried blocking the phone as a strategy to put distance between us, but this only resulted in him leaving a message, being as sweet and understanding as he could be and seeming confused as to why I needed to block him. He also was sweet and gentle with me, which did not make ending things any easier.

What I needed to remember at the time—but did not because of the heart strings connecting myself to him—"*is God is not the author of confusion*" (paraphrased 1 Corinthians 14:33 KJV). I would feel inhumane to not respond. Then around the mountain we would go again because I was concerned about not adding more hurt to the already very painful situation we were both in. This desire to not hurt him only prolonged our dysfunctional bond and the inevitable pain we would both experience in parting ways.

The guilt of doing or not doing was something else I realized had been planted in me as a child. My parents, who were consumed with alcoholism, thought it was right to criticize everything. Both of my parents were very distrustful of each other and most everyone else. They didn't like my friends, no matter what they were into. In all honestly, I had friends who were involved in both light and darkness before I truly understood the difference was spiritual in nature. A lot of those behaviors even at the time I justified as kids being kids. However, now as an adult behaving more like a teen, I had to look back and see what past experiences were fueling this blatant foolishness in my life. What need from back then was I trying on my own to meet rather than waiting and allowing God's will to be done.

Upon reflection, what was really needed was some adult guidance in what was righteous. My guess is my mom's heart and mind had been swallowed up by some of the perceived voids from her past as well. I do recall her saying that she felt as though her mom wasn't around, due to being at work all the time. This could have been an indication of my mom not feeling valued or worthy of quality time. Also, the fact my grandad was an alcoholic can cause a whole host of internalized issues, abandonment, lack of emotional support, and denial of reality, to name a few.

There was also this dark, looming reality that took a while to uncover. I made up my mind somewhere along life's path that having a man and a committed relationship would somehow make me better than my mom who, as far as I know, never desired to have a long-term committed relationship to a man. This was a belief I had to confess and repent for having.

This was also the time I realized these generational curses need to stop. I needed to acknowledge, more often than not, I was trying to be the change rather than submitting all this first and foremost to the Author and Finisher of not only faith but also our love story. Now I could more clearly see the plank in my own eye and ask the Lord Jesus to remove it and give me right vision according to His Word. No more examining the wreckage of the past, but now I could be diligent to co-operate with God the promising future promised in His Word.

Believing to Pity Someone
is to Love Them

There was this deeply rooted belief from my childhood that correlated pity and love. This was an unspoken reality with my mother as I watched alcoholism change her into someone who could not be trusted. This was a woman who became hard to respect because of the choices she made. This is not to mention the anxiety, the worry, and confusion I felt regarding what had happened to the woman, my mother, who was previously so loving, so kind, and so consistent. The fact someone said she was sick stayed with me. I didn't quite understand the origin of the sickness as a child but did conclude anyone in their right mind most likely wouldn't choose this kind of life that revolved around consuming large amounts of alcohol and the dangers that resulted. It took years in therapy for me to come to a place of acceptance with my mother's choices, to forgive and find ways to honor and love her for the many positive ways she shaped my life.

Upon reflection, I understood how the grief and pain caused me to momentarily relapse in loving someone not yet saved because I felt bad for his loss of our baby. I wanted to make it easier on him, definitely not harder. Doing caring things for him seemed to be healing for me in a momentary sense yet I did not fully grasp that I was continuing to hurt myself along the way by allowing a continual wedge to come between me and God by holding on to someone outside of His will. This relationship with God was my most valued relationships, As a child, my relationship with my mother was my most valued relationship. Her sin got between her and me, her idolatry of alcohol combined with self-pity. Now here I was repeating this cycle with my sin coming between God and me...

Thankfully, now the light of God's truth was on it. Neither he nor she was ever to be first in my life, but God needed to be!

Sometimes I wonder if these instances of past powerlessness can become a snare for us to take the wheel of our life from God, resulting in us straying from His will for us. Do we subconsciously choose people where similar themes exist and try harder to have a different outcome? This is a self-imposed will versus the surrendered life to the will Christ Jesus has for us.

The thoughts uncovered while in prayer were these: While I was unable to remain connected to my yet-to-be-saved mother (faith declaration) in her alcoholism, I was able to remain connected to this yet-to-be-saved man and believed I could have a positive contribution to his life because he was still coming around. After giving me some time and space, he continued to check in and come back. This was one man who was not abandoning me, however I have since come to realize any relationship where sin is even an ongoing temptation is not worth hurting my relationship with Jesus, and therefore I had to let go.

Reflection Questions

Do you ever feel like you will lose in either decision you make? Explain:

What decision can you make that will bring you closer to God and honoring His Word in obedience?

What are the first steps to take in walking that decision out?

What areas do you need leadership, guidance, support, or mentorship in?

I needed a life-giving Scripture, along with accountability, to set me free from this bondage and this is what was discovered...

"Forasmuch then as Christ hath suffered for us in the flesh, arm yourselves likewise in the same mind: for he that hath suffered in the flesh hath ceased from sin; That he no longer should live the rest of his time in the flesh to the lusts of men, but to the will of God" (1 Peter 4:1-2 KJV).

What life-giving Scripture can give you victory over your situation?

_____

Perceived Voids

God created light to be separate from the darkness. Prior to there being light, the Word in Genesis 1:2-3 describes *"the earth as without form and void"* due to the darkness. This is a parallel of our lives prior to Christ and after in the illumination of His truth! We are without form (not yet in the potter's hand) and void, often attempting to fill ourselves with any and everything the world deems of value, chasing these things in hopes of finding lasting satisfaction only to discover it's all a grand illusion. The void within us remains until we recognize the need for unconditional love, hope beyond the grave, and One that is steady and does not change.

The void must be filled with biblical truth, which is our eternal foundation, so there is no pitfall to fall into. With the truth of God's Word there is no ignorance where we are looking to the world, people, or ideal circumstances to fill us.

Being human, we often look to things and people to fulfill our greatest needs, to soothe our emotions, and to supply some of what we perceive we are lacking. I was sure that having a consistent family, a husband, children, receiving motherly love and giving motherly love were the key to my contentment, but I discovered that they can be perceived voids. What I am hoping is for you to recognize all you need is found in Christ. The Word of God declares, *"and our own completeness if now found in Him. We are completely filled with God as Christ's fullness overflows within us"* (Colossians 2:10 TPT). He is all sufficient! What an assurance!

In the next section, I will share what my former beliefs were according to the world, which could also be referred to as my early BC programming. In the second part of the book, FORTIFIED FAITH, I will share what is actually true according to the Word of God. This is an example you can follow in identifying what your perceived voids are and then applying the light of God's Word, also known as the sword of the Spirit, to defeat the lies.

Family

I was born into a broken family with two parents who were not together after my first year of life; going between them at a distance was my norm. I have often said it felt like being a ping pong ball going back and forth.

At the age of fifteen, I was placed in a group home. From there I went to a friend's family who became foster parents for me. This was the first time I experienced what a family was like after my mom's boyfriend of seven years had left. After being in the midst of a functional family who loved God, there began my desire to adopt a Chinese girl. This was during the time of the one child law in China. I had a heart for orphans, feeling in a sense an orphan myself. My hope was to be present for a child so she would know she was loved and belonged just like this family attempted to do for me. Being there for someone else would help me have a greater sense of purpose, and although not every family is traditional, love and intention could make a difference in the life of those who were without parents.

My family did not know the truth from the Bible or what it meant to have a personal relationship with God. They were not encouraging, supportive, or there in times of critical need. They were primarily focused on themselves and survival. Momentarily soothing their emotional, mental, and physical pain was all they really knew to cope and something I would later walk through personally although I very much intended not to.

Husband

I wanted a man to love me in gentle ways, which was contrary to my earliest memories of my dad in his dealings with my mom. I desired a man who could keep his word, be consistent in the day to day interactions, providing security, safety, and protection. I also hoped for a man to lead with integrity.

A man is more often less emotional, which can be greatly stabilizing to a woman who is sensitive and feels everything deeply, including the feelings of others. He can be her place of steady refuge, to be held in his arms as the two breathe together and relax in spite of all that's unknown. A man can be a calming refuge as two hearts beat as one.

After asking the Lord to do a deep, thorough search in my heart and mind, He revealed to me that because no man ever committed himself to marrying my mother, it became ever more important to take that opportunity when it became available. A husband in the home of my upbringing was a missing piece of my life puzzle and now is a definite must for my future family.

This was an unhealed part of my past. I'm not sure if my mom chose not to get married to get a welfare check instead, but in a way it was a false assurance for me of being better than her to have a husband.

Children

Having children seemed like a blessing that would be beyond me. This was why at a young age, my first decision pertaining to the future was to adopt. When becoming pregnant did happen, in my first marriage, it seemed like it could be a corrective experience in every way. I vowed within to provide for the next generation all I did not have. Needless to say, when that did not go as planned, greater disappointment ensued. I learned through experience it is one thing to have the vision for a healthy, loving family, yet the roadmap of how to get there and a lot of healthy role modeling and support is still needed. Without a godly roadmap, we are still following the only roadmap we have ever had, all the while vainly hoping to not repeat what we have learned from our own family's dysfunction.

In my walk with Christ, after many grave mistakes regarding my own children, God has blessed me to be in the children's ministry at church. This was a position I had to step down from when I admitted my backslidden condition to my church mother. It was another area of deep woundedness to admit to her that I had succumbed to less than God's best regarding God's covenant plan for marriage. His blessed plan is for a woman to be obediently wed with a man with whom she is equally yoked and who is most definitely saved. This is the first step prior to having children. Too often children are being created to fill perceived voids versus understanding the necessary ingredients of being a successful family unit in God's eyes. I know because I did that very thing, somewhat subconsciously and somewhat aware.

In losing my position in the youth ministry, more grief ensued.

Recognizing my choices had far greater impact than on me alone; it was another area of profound loss. I pondered for a while about what happened to my gratitude unto God? I thought, how could I forget all He had done for me? It was because His Word was not before my face, rather I was staring off in confusion, wanting a man to come and bandage my heart. All the while I was neglecting the fact the Great Sheperd had carried me through more than a few storms and would carry me again as soon as I entered back into His loving arms.

Fun

Fun in my childhood seemed to be cut short. When my mom's drinking and drug use took off, it was time for me to be responsible and begin working and taking care of the home. There was no after-school recreation, and unfortunately even school and learning, which were previously my sanctuary, had become more of a time to distract myself from my home life. After school, work and keeping our home clean and organized became the primary focus.

Also, doing what my peers were doing to fit in became second nature. In hindsight, I realize my peer group was very influential, which my parents also warned against— Since they weren't making better choices themselves it was easy to justify not taking their advice and just going with the peer flow. As teens it is easy to tell ourselves our parents don't understand and believe that our "friends" are the experts on how to live in this time and day.

Greatest Longing– Being Mothered and Mothering

Not being able to be physically present for my own children is a story for another book. This separation between myself and both my daughters and fulfilling the role as their mother was the biggest perceived void in my life. This separation ultimately was due to the generational cycles continuing in my first marriage and my total ignorance to the reality of them, being young and completely unexperienced with spiritual realities. I was desperate to give them a together family rather than them being in a broken one; it was my main objective, not knowing at the time only Jesus Christ can hold two willing individuals together.

My mom was my whole world as a little girl. I have no early memories of her being harsh or unloving. I remember the first time she disciplined me around the age of five, when she asked if I had eaten some candy. I told her no, and she told me the importance of telling the truth in maintaining trust in our relationship. She took time to teach me to read and write before I entered kindergarten. We made cookies so many times together that I had remembered the recipe for a book we made in school for Mother's Day in kindergarten. She had me on a very consistent schedule which provided an assurance of her love.

When I was in second grade, my mom went to treatment for alcoholism. As a young girl, they told me my mom was sick. Although she was sober for a period of time, she went back to drinking. My mother was not able to care for herself or regulate her own emotions and therefore was unable to tend to mine. My mother is still alive, but I am not sure where. Last I heard she was doing some heavy drugs on top of the previous twenty years of drinking. To say how this has impacted me, well it would take another book, truth be told.

It is helpful to identify both your strengths and weaknesses in your Christian walk in order to have your faith fortified upon the Rock, who is also the Word. These areas could serve to drive prayer, to seek wise Christian counsel, and to ask God to reveal His truth in these areas. The following areas I have identified as my weak areas needing to be fortified in faith.

These are now surrendered areas. I am fully trusting the Lord to be my strength, my completion, and that He and I will co-labor in fortifying my faith to live in ways that are pleasing to Him. By the help and aid of the Holy Spirit I am committed to walking in greater obedience.

I have noticed some repeated times of stumbling in the past which indicate these are times to be alert to. Times of greater vulnerability include times of transition: moving to a new place, beginning a new job (especially something good), an answer to prayer, and a new territory to reflect the goodness of God. In these times especially, I have noticed the past seems to come in like a flood, attempting to wash me off the new ground in which God has blessed me to stand.

In previous times of grief and loss, the thought spiral begins as I contemplate how short life is, what is still broken and missing. These thoughts are often accompanied by nearly every emotion, taking me on a toxic tailspin into the past.

TO FORTIFIED FAITH

Applying the Word of Truth

Lighting Up the Perceived Voids...

All these perceived voids pertain to my past. Now, in order to fortify my faith, I needed to diligently replace percieved voids with biblical truth. Transformation comes by renewing my mind as written in Romans 12:2 TPT, "Stop imitating the ideals and opinions of the culture around you but be inwardly transformed by the Holy Spirit through a total reformation of how you think. This will empower you to discern God's will as you live a beautiful life, satisfying and perfect in His eyes."

These areas of longing, lack, and looking back will continually attempt to pull me back in if I am not trusting by faith in God to make all things new. Now that these times of greater vulnerability have been identified, I need to take new action. Otherwise, I will continue to return to my default program ingrained within. Along with the renewed mind, I must walk in faith that I am already healed from these past wounds and hurts, otherwise the emotions surrounding these areas will continue to dominate, especially in emotionally turbulent times.

As a child of God, I am thankful for the realization this cannot and should not continue to be so. My roots need to be deeper when the storms of life come. The Lord has equipped you and me with the tools to overcome. Identify these personal areas for you, renew your mind with a specific Word regarding those areas, and stand firm in faith.

As I spoke to my church mother the other day, she reminded me to think of these areas as doors the enemy is lurking behind, how these doors need to be guarded with the Word (sword found in Ephesians 5:17b) coupled with faith (Ephesians 5:16). The practical application of this concept can be found in the gospel accounts of Matthew 12:29 and Mark 3:27.

When you use the sword of the Spirit, which is the Word of God, you will be on the offensive side of the battle with the shield of faith to quench the fiery darts the enemy shoots your way. When emotions attempt to flood the mind, may the eye of faith clearly see your entire spiritual body stand firm in the eternal Word of God. The Word declares *"Where there is no vision, the people perish..."* (Proverbs 29:18 KJV) so it is

vital to take time and see yourself completely IN HIM!

Pause for a moment.

How can you see yourself completely in Christ?

What mental image comes to mind when you imagine this?

Seeing myself seated in the heavenly realm and seated at His right hand reminds me of the victory already won. This also fills me with great gratitude and thanksgiving because I know for certain it was Him who helped me and definitely not something done on my own.

While we identify and recognize the areas of brokenness in our lives, it is important to counter with the truth of God's Word. Even when you do not see the promise fulfilled yet, stand on God's word in faith, trusting fully He will bring it to pass.

"So shall my word be that goeth forth out of my mouth; it shall not return unto me void, but it shall accomplish that which I please, and it shall prosper in the thing whereto I sent it" (Isaiah 55:11 KJV).

Family

My family and upbringing had a great amount of dysfunction and brokenness, yet there were times of connection and fun. After my grandmother died, my family became more divided, then as time passed the Lord slowly began to bless me with a family in Christ.

"God setteth the solitary in families..." (Psalm 68:6a KJV)

"...having predestined us unto the adoption of children by Jesus Christ to himself, according to the good pleasure of His will, to the praise and glory of His grace, wherein He made us accepted IN the beloved" (Ephesians 1:5 KJV, emphasis added).

During the grieving and a recent move the physical, distance between my family in Christ and I had expanded. It was as though a spiritual amnesia came over me, and the default programming began. This was the default program of dealing with emotions alone. I urge you not to allow the enemy to isolate you in times of grief and/or emotional processing.

If you have yet to receive a new family in Christ, the first thing is to begin praying and believing for this family to be a reality. It may also require you take uncomfortable steps of attending a Bible study and, in time, being vulnerable with someone you can trust about your need of mentorship. Reaching out and sharing is where my journey of new life in Christ began. In all honesty, now that my focus is right, it is clear to see that. He has blessed me beyond measure with a

family in Christ much bigger than I had hoped or imagined.

My problem was I wasn't reaching out to them for prayer and was wallowing in the grief and suffering alone.

Grieving the loss of my grandmother was a time in which I made a very healthy decision to stop drinking, but this was followed by a very poor decision of allowing my abusive ex-husband in. Another one of the major downfalls at this time early in my Christian walk was not having an accountability partner. At the time, the emotional intoxication of hope was overriding the traumatic experiences I had with him.

My deep desire to prevent my own children's growing up in a broken home led me to reenter a dangerous situation with familiar spirits that was not ordained by God. Upon reflection, it is clear to see the areas of grief and loss had been a great stumbling block and therefore need to be deeply fortified in preparation of the future. This again confirms in times of great transition and emotional vulnerability, the enemy was lurking outside my door.

If you look at the patterns of families in the Bible, God has always worked in unconventional ways. May we understand that God does not use cookie cutter family situations but rather often works in mysterious ways.

Husband

Did you know the Word of God says Christ is our husband, and also that He is married to the backslider?

"For thy Maker is thine husband; the Lord of hosts is his name; and the Redeemer the Holy One of Israel; The God of the whole earth, shall He be called." Isaiah 54:5 KJV

How awesome is that truth!

He is our husband, and also the God of the whole earth! Let's talk about honor and reverence given unto Him; the Holy One! The One whose love can encompass the entire earth and all His inhabitants.

"Turn O backsliding children, saith the Lord; for I am married unto you…" Jeremiah 31:14a

One of the things that grieved my heart so deeply in this sin pattern was the adultery to my covenant marriage to the Lord, first and foremost. It grieved me to think that after all God had done for me, honoring Him is the very least I can do. Even when I am down and out, weighed down by emotions, He remains faithful and true. I am so grateful to have recommitted myself in purity, fully recognizing He will also be the one to help me remain that way. He will reveal and cleanse as needed. So now when that longing for a husband comes to my mind, I simply remind myself, the best Husband is already mine, available 24/7, and who knows me better than I know myself. He is intimately acquainted with me through and through, promising never to leave us but to continue loving us through this life to the next…faithfully bringing you and I into all the truth. His truth sets us free.

Children

"Your pure faith and love rest over your heart as you nurture those who are yet infants."

(Song of Songs 4:5 TPT)

What I desperately needed was a renewal of my mind regarding children in the sense of how we see them in the world. I needed to know and understand how God was going to use my life may not mean having biological children of my own to have and to raise. There are many lives we encounter, and with those encounters there are opportunities to model something new given by Jesus Christ. He created us all with measures of different qualities.

As I write this book, I am praying those who read it will choose His way and fortify their faith, to grow the fruit of patience while they wait, holding fast the Word of truth and trusting it to come to pass for their future children, whether biological, spiritual, or both.

When I was born again, I needed spiritual parents to teach and model to me the ways of God. When we teach others as God as taught us, we become in a sense spiritual parents. My niece will have the privilege of knowing both the kingdom of God and the word while she grows in who God called her to be.

Fun

This is the type of fun inspired by a childlike joy and where wonder and awe in God and His goodness abounds. It is fun to worship, to feel the presence of God and hear His voice. It is fun to randomly speak to a stranger of the goodness of our God. It is fun to give and to bless, knowing God has blessed me with the privilege of making another smile, and to know they are loved and cared for. It is fun when He sends a new song from heaven, although I'm not particularly gifted in singing. It is fun to see all of the intricate details in His wondrous creation all around us. It is fun to create as our Abba, Daddy, has created in many forms of artistic expression. It is fun to be watchful of the changing sky, of the birds flying by, especially the golden finch, as He lovingly knows it is my favorite one…

How do you experience fun?

Mothering and Being Mothered

God has blessed me with many spiritual mothers. These are mothers who pray, who lead godly lives, whether married, divorced, or widowed. The most important quality is that they love beyond measure. They are of various ages and skin complexions. They have various gifts, talents, and measures of faith. Some have traveled internationally doing ministry. I am very blessed indeed to have these mothers who know my past, present, and speak the life-giving word of God into my future.

Truth be told, a major reason this book has been written is due to the prophetic words of my spiritual mothers, their encouragement and affirmation of what God has placed inside of me.

The very first church God brought me to be an active member of, the First Lady and the Pastor confirmed I am a writer from the previous letters I had written to them, prior to us meeting in person. The first lady handed me one of many books she had published and said, "If God can do it through me, He can also do it in you." This gave me a great sense of purpose in a time of transition. It was a much needed encouragement in the gift God had placed inside.

Another spiritual mother He blessed me with on the block across the street from me declared, "Many books are inside of you, and you will write to the glory of the King." She actually went on to glory as this book was being written, which demonstrates the reality that prophetic words can outlive us in the generations to come.

Defined Values

Standing on biblical truth you and I believe, particularly in times of transition or emotional distress, is one of the greatest strategies God has given me as I move forward on my journey. This is because in these times, focus on truth is going to be required when the storms and lies of the enemy attempt to bombard your thoughts and life.

It is necessary to get clarity about what Scriptures will be an anchor in times of hardship to stand firm in the truth of God: our everlasting foundation. The first truth I have embraced is knowing and remembering that *"I am healed by His stripes"* (paraphrased Isaiah 53:5) from all that past dysfunction and familiarity with sin. This healing applies to not just physical well-being but mental and emotional as well.

Yes, I may experience some heartbreak due to grief or loss, but the Lord promises also to be close to those who are broken and contrite in spirit (paraphrased Psalm 34:8). For my family who is yet to be saved, the Word says to *"Believe in the Lord Jesus and you will be saved – along with everyone in your household"* (Acts 16:31 NLT). In radical faith, I trust that praying for salvation of others applies to any and everyone who lives in any house the Lord has blessed, and will bless me to set my foot in. Just like the salvation verse I shared,

there is a promise or word for every experience we could face. The question is, will you be responsible to search out the Word of truth to illuminate the dark areas of your life? To wield your sword and stand firm in His Word as your shield of faith when the trials of life come?

Generational Patterns

Examining the generational patterns of your parents and other relatives may help you recognized patterns you are repeating, but be aware that Christ is a bondage breaker. I will discuss patterns I have observed within different relationships throughout my life.

Please, men and women of God, stand for Christ, being firm in your resolve regarding what it is you know God has for you, no matter what your past has held. My past was an extremely broken one. My mother was an alcoholic and pushed the best man she had away when I was around eleven years of age. I never emotionally processed this loss because logically I attributed it as a result of my mother's alcoholism. The effects of her drinking somehow also caused me to not feel worthy of a good man as I grew into a young lady. Her emotional stuntedness became mine as well. This was baggage passed down that I unconsciously accepted rather than rejected. I was completely unaware that there was even an option for better until I admitted a far more desperate need for Christ at the age of twenty-seven.

Prior to the time of him leaving, I had witnessed neighbors and some friends harshly judge my mom for her drinking. My family had their thoughts and opinions, and fingers pointed at others to blame, which were often my dad, my mom's dad, or my grandpa. This was something at a young age I did not want to do; judge someone's outward behavior to determine if they were worthy of being loved and treated well. It was as though at a young age I knew there was something deeper at work within my mom, that there was a solution to her issue that was going to have to be beyond people...

During this time, my thoughts or feelings regarding my mom were never investigated or examined. Never having seen true vulnerability, or the sharing of truth in a way that did not include blame or accountability from the person speaking, left me with some ineffective models of operation. The main one was stuffing all my true feelings down and feeling insignificant to share the actual matters of my heart. There was so much shame I carried but wasn't even aware at the time what shame was.

When I was twelve, a friend I went to school with and I were in her kitchen at the time, and she introduced me to Jesus.

She said He loved me enough to die for my sins. My mouth fell to the floor. I readily accepted Him as my Savior, because love coupled with sacrifice was not a concept I had ever known before.

At the age of seventeen, I began seeing this really sweet and gentle guy who was very responsible, kind, and caring. He wasn't like the other guys I had known, who upon reflection could be referred to as street guys. What I mean by street guys are literally ones running the streets, drinking, smoking, basically aimless with no goals or ambitions in sight except to "kick it," a term we used in the '90s.

This guy was respectful towards his mom and his sister, went to school and worked a job. He would pick me up from school every day even though he attended a different school. We worked together, so when one of my co-workers told me he was serious about me, I ran away from him as fast as possible. By this time, I already began feeling unworthy of someone who actually had consistency to offer. I recall him bringing me to his house and everything was white, clean, and very orderly. It was in that very moment stepping into his home that the comparisons began. In my home everything was brown and smoke stained, no matter how much washing of the walls I did. It was clear to see his mom maintained a high level of cleanliness, order within her home, and took good care of her two children. My mom had been unable to keep steady employment, often sleeping into the afternoon after being out drinking the night before. I became the keeper of the home while she was either sleeping or drinking. In all honesty we would have been homeless if it weren't for my grandparents whom my mom rented from when she had money to pay.

When she didn't, they graciously allowed us to remain.

My grandma found out about my boyfriend from my mom and didn't want me to date him because he was of another race. She threatened to cancel Thanksgiving, which didn't matter to me. I thought, if only she knew skin color had nothing to do with character. But after her judgment of him, and as I began to compare our lives, it became clear he would be way better off without me and all my family instability, better off without witnessing their inaccurate judgements and personal accountability.

After breaking it off with him, I sunk into a deeper sense of unworthiness. It seemed I was drawn to others who also believed themselves to be unworthy, who were not actively working towards any goals, with no ambitions, and just coasting through life. I did, however, have goals buried down inside and very much wanted something different and better. I just did not know faith and didn't know the Word of God, so the surrounding undercurrent of the world was slowly but surely dragging me in.

Being one hundred percent honest, relationships have been a huge stumbling block and the men I choose or allowed into my life would most likely be the reason why. These are men that I hoped to bring from darkness to light, from bondage to freedom, to new life in Christ Jesus, but had yet to surrender to His great love.

This pattern of fornication, confession, and repentance would happen more times than I care to admit, but now that it is realized, the only man for me will recognize his and my value is found in the sacrificial offering of Jesus Christ, who paid it all. Jesus, who by His willing death on the cross, declared you and me were worth Him giving up His very life. This was not only to give us heaven but to also enable us to bring heaven here while we walk the earth, just as He did.

When you realize a man is not on the same page, please do not be carried away on the wings of hope. While it is great to pray for others to experience salvation, to shine the light of your personal salvation, primarily I encourage you to flee. Women often have a heart to see the best, but the man has to be moving in that direction, otherwise you will be following him back to Egypt, and this is because God wired men to lead and women to follow. There are only two directions: forward into the Kingdom of God and freedom or back into Egypt, which is bondage. It is a dishonor to God when we attempt to do things any other way.

As a matter of fact, Eve deciding to follow a voice that was not God's, or follow her husband's lead, turned the very world upside down. This voice was of course Satan's. I have learned time and time again following someone who is not following God will bring discipline. If you have lived any amount of time and honestly examine yourself, I am certain you will also discover this to be true. Let us choose better. God's way is best! Being obedient to His commands has many benefits found also in the Word.

Desire is a fleshly and powerful tie between two individuals. Desire, in multiple areas, can become a stronghold. In regards to the man with whom I shared a baby, I noticed that my emotional dependence upon him after losing the baby became stronger. I am not sure if it was because of the bonding hormones a mother produces or just the fact that no man had comforted me in a previous time of devastation, but it was clear my heart and mind were in a battle.

This battle on one hand involved a long list of all the biblical reasons clarifying why we would not have a future together, but my heart countered this long list with a single verse, "love keeps no record of wrongs," which is also biblical. My mind would say, "well you can love him from a distance like you have had to do many times before," and my heart would argue, "I can't lose another person right now, not after six deaths, including our baby and the living separation with my mom and my two daughters." Clearly it was selfishness and ultimately holding on to someone who would need to change allegiances from the god of this world to the God of Heaven above. Also, I needed to honestly address what this choice to not let go was saying about my own allegiance.

It became clear I was in a losing battle with myself. In past times of great difficulty, support groups had been helpful, so I joined a co-dependency anonymous group. I also still needed the *"prayers of the righteous to availeth much"* (James 5:16) on my behalf. I knew the peace of God prior to this warfare and wanted that desperately again. It required being vulnerable in my weaknesses with others who knew the only true source of our strength with Him being our ability to overcome temptation and the one who makes the way of escape we must take.

"Hope deferred
makes the heart sick..."

One of the greatest entryways into my heart where outside temptations have overcome what I know to be true is during the times when it seems as if God is not coming through on my timetable. This is also known as impatience, particularly when grief strikes. My mind will begin to remember how short life is, how important it is to make the moments count, and what currently is missing, particularly concerning valuable relationships.

This is when the enemy begins whispering lies, and my mind can easily make comparisons which appear as though God is unfair. This is very same lie from the beginning of time between Eve and the serpent.

This is something I now recognize and will have to boldly declare verses related to the eternal Word of God so my emotions and flesh are not permitted to be dominated, which is an open door to the enemy's lies. I also have to remind myself either I am drawing from a bitter well of the world's experience or drawing from a well of living waters.

This option of which well you will draw from can ever be a reminder of His well of living waters always being available, and that the choice is yours and mine to make. The enemy continually wants to point us back to the old, contaminated well, yet Jesus beckons us deeper into His well of everlasting life. Sometimes the emotional storms of life will cloud the reality: His well is still there, still eternal, and still promising that when we drink from it we will never thirst again.

This momentary spiritual blindness was one of the biggest deceptions I experienced in this recent downfall. Had I viewed my apartment as the peaceful sanctuary in which God truly blessed it to be, as a set apart place, a place of refuge and rest, a place prayed and desired for a very long time, I would have treated it as such. If I had been able to get present it would have been clear He had provided all my needs and had healed me to be where I was that day just as He had promised.

This is why waiting and shelving desire is better and guarding my heart is essential when I begin to weary in doing, good which the Bible also commands us not to do. As my pastor reminds us, the Lord makes a way of escape so when you recognize you are cornered in that place, beginning to be bombarded with lies, look for the nearest exit. *"He is the door!"* (paraphrased John 10:7.) Enter into Him, in His wounds; He endured for you! And remember you are already healed and this is when we need to renew our mind according to His truth and reject any and all lies.

Encourage yourself with Scripture…

Growing the Fruit of Patience AKA Longsuffering

If you have ever encountered a person who is patient with you, it is such a refreshing experience to behold, especially if you encountered many people who did not have it. This is a refreshing quality because it is a fruit of the Holy Spirit. It is an area I have been most challenged with. By faith, I believe it is definitely evident in my life, but there are too many times where my flesh momentarily won, and the enemy attempted to convince me it never was really there to begin with. These times come when I am exhausted, not eating well, or when emotional storms come.

Take a moment to visualize God's great patience towards us. How His mercy endures and how He refuses to give up on us when we will so readily give up on others when they are not living up to our expectations. At other times, we may feel like giving up on ourselves.

When I visualize myself as a tree of His righteousness and patience being a fruit of His Spirit within,I may not always feel it, yet His truth is He has given it. Galatians 5:22 Let your faith see this in advance and be brought to your remembrance in the time of greatest need as you draw on this eternal truth and spiritual root.

When I looked to the Word to fortify my faith, these were the Scriptures that really spoke to me!

Now may the God who brought us peace by
raising from the dead our Lord Jesus
Christ so that he would be the Great
Shepherd of His flock, and by the power
of the blood of the eternal covenant
may He work perfection into every
part of you by giving you all you need
to fulfill your destiny. And may He
express through you all that is excellent
and pleasing to Him, through your life
union with Jesus the Anointed One
who is to receive all glory forever.

Hebrews 13:20-21 TPT

Dealing with Loneliness

Upon prayer and examination, times of perceived loneliness have been especially vulnerable for me. Once I realized this reality, it was equally clear I needed a new perspective on this emotion. When closely examining the life of Jesus, He also had to be incredibly lonely due to His understanding that most, even those closest to Him, did not understand the purpose and plan God sent Him to the earth to accomplish. So what did Jesus do? He relied on His heavenly Father, and this is exactly what I need to emulate with His help, when the perceived void of loneliness arises.

He also understood that His time on earth was short. He was here for a predestined purpose and He knew whom He would be returning back to. May we remember also our times of loneliness, of perceived separation, this life here is a limited time offer. First the Holy Spirit promises to be with us until the return on Christ. Second we can remember that one day we will be embraced eternally by Him. May the longing we feel at times be an assurance of what is to come.

Conflicting Natures

It is important to be aware of the conflicting nature of the flesh and ask Jesus if a relationship conflicts with your relationship with Him. Our most life-giving relationship will always be with Christ. Our flesh attempts to battle God's Spirit within each of us. A man without God is only flesh, so in a simple mathematical concept, it becomes two fleshly appetites working against the spirit of God, as our flesh doesn't die when we become born again but something we must crucify daily. This was why Jesus said, *"Watch and pray so that you fall not into temptation. The Spirit is willing but the flesh is weak"* (Matthew 26:41 NIV).

This is why mutual agreement in the Word and being in a relationship with Christ is essential for both individuals who are committed to walking together through life. Otherwise, you are going to be in a relationship feeling alone and as though you are battling the One whom you are supposed to be walking alongside. Also, there is the potential to hinder your relationship with God, which is the last thing we want to do. We want to have someone in which we can continue moving forward versus battling our flesh and the flesh of another, which I can assure you, will not work.

The Bible says, *"That ye put off concerning the former conversation the old man, which is corrupt according to its deceitful lusts; and be renewed in the spirit of your mind; And that ye put on the new man, which after God is created in righteousness and true holiness"* (Ephesians 4:22-24 KJV).

Guarding the Heart

"Every word of God is pure; He is a shield unto them that put their trust in Him." Proverbs 30:5

Lately I have been saying this out loud, "Lord, I do not understand what's going on, but I trust you." This has mostly been pertaining to situations others are experiencing. In all honesty, this relates to the processing of my emotions as well. It is important to continually renew my mind remembering that the burden to figure everything out is not mine. Life situations that surround me are not always for me to understand but to redirect my heart and mind to the One who knows and sees all.

"Trust in the Lord with all thine heart, lean not unto thine own understanding. In ALL your ways acknowledge Him and He will direct your path." Proverbs 3:5-6 KJV

This verse is especially important because one of the reasons I was struggling to guard my heart is due to the lack of protection being a norm throughout my childhood. Then that lack of safety continued into my first marriage, which is also the topic of another book. It took a while, yet when I sought the Lord, He showed me my heart was His treasure and therefore valuable. That ultimately our hearts belong to Him when we are born again and are worthy of protecting…

Intimacy with God

Looking back on where the indiscretion began, it is now clear to see the broken places were creating some sort of emotional riptide pulling me into the past rather than the previous genuine hope for my future in the Lord Jesus Christ. The old and familiar was the default in contrast to the new thing I had so often experienced the Lord Jesus doing. So how do we deal with the broken areas that still exist within? How do we stand firm when all of the past heartaches seem to flood over us once again?

First of all, I think we need to have a honest heart to heart with the Lord and make this an ongoing pattern.

"Join me everyone! Trust only in God every moment! Tell Him your troubles and pour out your heart longings to Him. Believe me when I tell you-He will help you!" (Psalm 62:8 TPT). There is always so much to remain grateful for. *"In everything, give thanks, for this is the will of God in Jesus Christ concerning you"* (1 Thessalonians 5:18 KJV). I focused on all that God delivered me from pertaining to my birth family, especially for giving me new life in Him. When I remember this, a great joy wells up inside of me.

I want to encourage you these are vitally important times to reach out to sisters and brothers in Christ who are solid in their faith and walking by the power of the Holy Spirit. There was and continues to be a sister in Christ I can call if company was a necessity. Yet somehow this man who I was familiar with in my past seemed to be my heart's desire in that moment.

Longing to laugh and reminisce, I convinced myself his company would be harmless. Looking back on that specific time, I realize my own negligence in protecting my heart. Guarding my heart meant protecting the biblical values and seeds of faith so lovingly planted there, like a fence around what is most precious.

This fence puts a safe barrier around the identity given to us by Christ and affirms who He made us to be. It safeguards the purpose He called us to fulfill for His Kingdom in testifying that the old life was gone and the new had come. This greater depth of understanding results in willfully choosing to live a life that glorifies Him. Upon reflection, it is now apparent this familiar spirit of worldly comfort can only appeal to an unguarded (vulnerable) heart or a mind not entirely grasping at the moment in time the reality of being made totally new in Christ. This newness includes the realization that our sins have been crucified in Christ and now only have the authority that we allow them to have in our flesh.

It was in this realization that it became clear I needed to take the whole matter more seriously, letting my "yes be yes and my no be no," (paraphrased from James 5:12) in protection of preserving God's best. The honest conversation with the Lord about any and all of the details of the tempting situation would most likely have sufficed, along with a good night's rest. Hindsight is 20/20, so now with great clarity regarding the hardships suffered, it will be important to remember these truths and apply them going forward. Do not allow the devil to disqualify you with any lies that God will not forgive. Get up quickly and back into the race!

Taking Every Thought Captive

We have two choices with every thought, to accept it or reject it. This is so critical to recognize. When I was younger, people used to say you cannot stop a bird from landing on you, but you can stop it from building a nest. This is the same for our thought life. Not every thought belongs in the mind of one "born again," therefore those thoughts must be rejected. We are "born again" because Jesus says in Him, we are a new creation however our mind needs to continually being renewed and transformed by His Word.

Being "born again" means new thinking is required, founded on the Word of God, in opposition to the former programming from the world. It means having a new nature that wants to be pleasing to God and having conviction when we do wrong to repent and seek His help in doing the new thing He has called us to.

On my ride home from work today I heard the voice of the Lord telling me, "I have always been there, Jess, when your mom was at the bar, and even while you are waiting for a man to truly love you the way I intend. I am here every moment, providing for your every need." The tears began to stream down my face because deep down in my heart, I knew this was so very true. The loving conviction then came. How often do I look to what is still remaining to be healed and mended by Him versus having sheer gratitude for all God has already done? Do you ever just take an honest evaluation of your life and are simply amazed at all the hardships Jesus brought you through? All the moments where you could have completely lost your mind, yet He kept you. It is so important to remember His faithfulness in times past and remain confident He is the same God to pull us through whatever we are currently facing. It is a sure reminder that only God could have given me the strength to survive those things. He is my strength now, and He will be my strength when it is time to endure again. The same is true for you and whatever situations you are currently facing and will face in the future. May our dependence be upon His proven faithfulness.

Kingdom Priorities

"Seek ye first the kingdom of God and His righteousness and all these things shall be added unto you." Matthew 6:33 KJV

In these instances of being carried away on the wings of hope regarding an unsaved man, my intentions seemed right and seemed loving. However underlying was just another idol of believing it's up to me to positively impact this person towards a better way of living.

If you and I never did anything more than pray for others, in instances where temptation is lurking, it would be enough. I truly believe this is the most pleasing thing to God to do. To remain in a safe place and trust by faith, *"The prayers of the righteous availeth much"* (James 5:16 KJV). We can rest in faith and assurance that when we pray according to His will, in His time, He will fulfill it. To surrender and trust Him above all else to do what He alone can do. When my thoughts become a list of what I can do, my expectation is not where it needs to be, and that is on Him.

"My soul, wait thou only upon God; For my expectation is from Him." Psalm 62:5 KJV

This is waiting on Him. How often will the enemy try to convince us to do something, to take an action, bringing us into harm's way. What we can do is pray, stay righteous, and trust by faith. Let us continue seeking His will to be done on this earth through faith and prayer...

The Word of God – Our Main Weapon

The armor of God is found in Ephesians 6:12-19 TPT with specific emphasis on verse 17-18. *"Embrace the power of salvation's full deliverance, like a helmet to protect your heart from lies. And take the mighty razor-sharp Spirit-sword of the spoken word of God."* Not knowing the Word of God, His truth and His promises are like going into a war with no weapon. All the benefits that come with the Word are too many for this book, so will focus on a few key areas.

Hearing, reading, and believing the Word is the only way we can begin renewing our mind. This renewal is essential in having a new, abundant life in Christ. We must study, chew on, and basically marinate in the Word of God. The enemy is very crafty in trying to sneak tiny lies or even partial truths into our minds. He is ever attempting to plant seeds of doubt and just as Jesus demonstrated, we are to battle him back in a truth-filled stance upon which we will need to stand fast on. Remember, He is the Rock upon which we stand. We must know that hearing and obeying the Word of God is described "as being a wise man, building your house on a rock." This means knowing and obeying the Word will keep you steady in times of emotional storms.

Faith comes by hearing the Word of God over and over. In order for those old tapes to continue playing, in order for those habits and patterns to be broken, we must prioritize His Word. This translation stated the *"spoken* Word," the hearing of ourselves speaking the Words that agree with heaven above. The reverberation of our mouths as the prophetic Word is coming forth is powerful. This is why the enemy wants shame to silence us. He is happy when we allow our flesh to dominate us in carnality because it renders us ineffective in the kingdom.

I encourage you to be creative in learning and memorizing the essential truths which are eternal.

Obedience Produces Confidence in God

The Word of God says, *"It is good for man not to touch a woman"* (1 Corinthians 7:1 KJV). I literally read this while still craving his embrace, so I sat with the Lord Jesus regarding this. It was clear to me why my church family states it is important to not be alone with a man. The Bible goes on to say, *"Nevertheless, to avoid fornication,"* the importance of a man having his own wife and a woman her own husband. It is clear the Lord is not in favor of casual relationships that have any physical component. My life experience can personally testify to this.

In my heart-to-heart with the Lord, He asked, "What do you think being held by a man signifies?" At first I felt embarrassed because in my heart and mind things tend to go so much deeper than the actual action. So after the embarrassment of wanting it to mean so much more to the man who last held me would attest, I wrote down just what it meant.

Being held by a man means for me there is a protective element, a sense of security and stability. Being held gives me the sense he has me blanketed in more ways than a physical covering. That he is covering me mentally, emotionally, and spiritually, and that this embrace symbolizes everything will be okay. This is because physical closeness could only occur when I felt extremely comfortable with someone, and when I trusted them not to hurt me. At a young age, my desire was for one man. The first man to hold me was who I wanted to also be the last. Can I tell you that is already true and will now continue to be? That man is Father God. He knit me in my mother's womb and will be the permanent loving embrace of eternity. We are sheltered under His wings every night and day.

Even after receiving this revelation from God, I was still struggling to let the guy go, and even this struggle pointed me back to God. Why did I continue to struggle with letting this man go, even though it was clear what God wanted me to do? This is the question I continued to ask myself. There are many answers to these questions, and they all seem to boil down to feelings and a lack of a consistent, ongoing, healthy attachment to a care-giver in my childhood. This was not something I could expect to be fixed by a man, especially not a man still in the world. It is important to take note as to what is surfacing so you can honestly pour your heart out to

God. Once the honest emotions are poured out, pray for wisdom, fully trusting Him for healing, deliverance, and the filling of every perceived void. The truth is He already has. The question is, do you believe it? If not, what is hindering your belief? Bring it all to Him and He will show you the way to freedom.

Recently I heard a sermon about carnality (allowing the flesh dominate more than His Spirit) being a killer of where God wants to take us. Knowing my faith and trust in God needs to be bigger than any fleshly desire has been the reminder on my heart this past week. *"He must increase and I must decrease"* (paraphrased John 3:30 KJV).

*"For a just man falleth seven times, and riseth up again."*Proverbs 24:16 KJV

The Benefits of Obedience

God and His will must become my priority. My trust is in God to grant me a greater desire for Him because of all the benefits (love, peace, confidence, and a clear conscience) that come with obedience. The first benefit is *"His perfect love casteth out all fear"* (1 John 5:18 KJV). The great peace that also comes with this reality is very much an experience that words cannot even begin to express. Perhaps because words are not needed when peace is present.

When I look back on the year of backsliding, confessing and being sorrowful but still returning to sin, a lot of fear began to creep into my life. These consequences of sin began to affect me in negative ways, in more ways than I can count. I thank God my mind was not turned over to a reprobate mind as the Word describes. I could still recount the goodness, joy, and peace that only He gives. God's peace is not something that the world and all its fleeting pleasures can provide. I am grateful the Lord was showing me how my flesh attempts to separate me from God with its momentary desires instead of keeping what is eternal at the forefront of my mind. This is why the Bible says in Galatians 5:24, *"And they that are Christ's have crucified the flesh with its affections and lusts.* " A crucified flesh is not being pulled into sin because it is dead.

My question moving forward is how will I be obedient today? I was determined to stay focused on writing this document and allow God to help me overcome the next trial and test. Submitting to His will result in greater authority for the winning of souls for the kingdom, for greater freedom for those that are saved, and ultimately His predestined purpose is so much greater than this wretched flesh of mine.

I have learned through experience there is nothing better than having a pure conscious before my Maker, Creator, Redeemer, and Faithful Friend.

Recognizing the Calling

"Now listen, daughter, pay attention, and forget about your past. Put behind you every attachment to the familiar, even those who once were close to you!" Psalms 45:10 TPT

Letting go has been very difficult for me due to my own experience of abandonment. I do not want to inflict the feelings that come with that on anyone else. There have been a number of times where I literally felt emotionally torn while praying for those I love to be saved and "born again." A dear sister in Christ gently let me know I had the gift of intercessory prayer. "What a gift!" she exclaimed as it seemed I was emotionally crumbling. Sometimes it is as though I can feel the weight of sin others are carrying while also personally knowing the bondage they are experiencing. I begin to cry out on their behalf to the God of all comfort, the God who draws near to the broken in heart and contrite in spirit. The enormity of it all helped me also recognize all the more why my heart must remain pure and protected, in order that *"the prayers of the righteous availeth much"* (James 5:16 KJV). So fully walking in His righteousness is the requirement, which requires a daily denial of the fleshly desires. A confession and repentance of wrong thoughts and attitudes will keep further wrong actions from taking place. In this denial of the flesh, we are able to walk in the authority that He has granted to you and I as His precious children.

Sometimes it is necessary to think a decision through as far as possible. If I decide, in a certain way, how will this look in six months, nine months, and two years. For example, when I considered how much I loved the man that I shared this baby with, thought about the fact that he said he believed God brought us together, and more importantly that Jesus is God's son, there was still the future to consider as well. Even after saying he wanted to marry me, his lifestyle was still the same. Believing in Jesus and choosing to live like Jesus are two different things. So with that, I had no other choice except to walk away.

A person can believe in Jesus but not be born again. The Bible says, *"You can believe all you want that there is one true God, that's wonderful! But even the demons know this and tremble with fear before Him, yet they are unchanged, they remain demons"* (James 2:19 TPT). His lack of salvation brought a deep fear into me, knowing if something fatal happened to him, I would share responsibility in him being eternally separated from God due to partnering in sinful actions with him although I shared the gospel. He also witnessed me have conviction regarding fornication, knowing it was not pleasing to God, and until he sought God for himself, he was still bearing the sin debt. This was compounded by the reality that so many people he knew were dying during the time we were together This made it especially difficult to walk away, for I too knew great loss.

"Draw near to God, and He will draw near to you. Cleanse your hands, ye sinners, and purify your hearts, ye double minded. Be afflicted and mourn and weep; let your laughter be turned to mourning and your joy to heaviness. Humble yourselves in the sight of the Lord, and He shall lift you up." James 4:8-10 KJV

One of the most stressful situations to be in as a "born again" believer is battling between the flesh and the Spirit of God, which is something we do not need to do when we agree with God that our flesh has been crucified with Christ. This was a vital belief I was neglecting during this period of time. After knowing His peace yet continuing to return to sin, then being deeply remorseful, this condition of the mind and heart is very disruptive to our relationship with the Heavenly

Father. It is important to keep in mind that this relationship has been made possible by the sacrifice of Christ.

To remember we are now to "present our bodies as a living sacrifice, which is our reasonable service...*by the mercy of God*" (Romans 12:1 KJV). We are not to momentarily satisfy the flesh only to be convicted immediately after and then regret once again allowing the flesh to dominate.

As I struggled to let go of this man, this relationship in which a future generation was cut short, to let go of the emotional connection we shared, the ways I felt seen and known by him, were areas my intimacy with Jesus needed to grow. My faith in Him had to fill this space. My faith had to look forward and stop looking back. My faith needed to grow in knowing through God His *"love never brings fear, for fear is always related to punishment. But love's perfection drives the fear of punishment far from our hearts"* (1 John 4:18 NIV). The fears that needed to be driven out were running out of time for a family (husband), for a baby, and for a lifelong companion. My intimacy with Christ needed to drown out the lies that say no one will love me, that I'll never be enough, and that I'll be a failure forever when it comes to a man.

A Word to the Wise

Another human being cannot be the keeper of your conscious. This is a personal job. This is why the Word of God says, *"Work out your own salvation with fear and trembling"* (Philippians 2:12 KJV). In my own walk, I have realized this can be that much more challenging because I had not been trained or led by those who had a moral compass desiring to please God. This meant forging a whole new pathway of something formerly not observed in both my heart and mind.

At first this can be very daunting and may actually seem impossible. The Word actually declares, *"With men this is impossible,"* yet the verse continues, *"but with God all things are possible"* (Matt. 19:26 KJV). This is God's truth. When we agree with His truth, we become overcomers! May we stand and boldly proclaim this truth, trusting the Lord to lead us and guide us every step of the way.

Prayer Unto God

Dearest Jesus,

Thank You that with You all things become possible! Thank You for all the areas You have already delivered us from that were not pleasing to You. Because of Your faithfulness in these areas, I trust You to be faithful in delivering me from this area of fornication, in this area of idolatry and adultery.

Show me how to love You fully and completely with the love You have shown me. Help me walk in a love that covers, a love that heals, a love that reflects an image of Your righteousness and that is perfect in all of Your ways. Help me embrace a love that forgives when I do not understand, but most importantly a love that will not run away but will run right into Your embrace! Thank You for Your love that teaches us, prunes us, and shapes us into someone completely new! In Jesus name we pray, amen!

Looking Forward in Faith

"Therefore we ought to give the more earnest heed to the things we have heard lest at any time we should let them slip." (Hebrews 2:1 KJV)

The Lord reminded me it was time to plan, to dream, to begin building again. Writing this book began the journey of having a new vision for the future, after a long season of grief and loss. Having done therapy during the this time and many years previously I became well acquainted with my past and began overanalyzing. This overanalyzing required me to set boundaries with my therapist as well. A time came where the past patterns had been clearly identified and it was no longer beneficial to continue looking back. Those chapters needed to be closed and a new future following God's Word needed to transpire. A shift in focus was necessary to become fully present in the moment, to be grateful and to embrace the opportunities God provides to plant seeds of love and truth in the lives of others.

I also needed to look forward to fulfilling some of the dreams God had given me. Guess what? These dreams were so much bigger than just a relationship with a man, but how to sow compassion into the lives of others. He understands everything we face and yet was without sin. Why? I believe one of many reasons was because He knew and embraced His purpose of being a loving sacrifice to redeem and restore. He came to earth not to satisfy His flesh but to redeem us. He remained focused on the end result from the very beginning. My trust is we will begin to do the same.

Now it is time to continue being obedient, planting seeds of love and filling my mind with the Word to fuel my faith in what is to come. Is it time for you to begin dreaming again?

What area do you feel a strong desire to contribute meaningfully in the lives of others?

Visual Representation of
Protecting the Heart

"Where there is no vision the people perish."(Proverbs29:18 KJV)

"Write the vision and make it plain on tablets,

that he may run that readeth it."(Habakkuk 2:2 KJV)

As I asked the Lord, "How do I protect my heart?" knowing there was an obligation for me to fulfill, I came across visual journaling activity on YouTube.

Although I did not do the journaling exercise in the same way they described, it was a tremendous tool in getting started. As the Lord needed to be my guide, I really took my time with this. Much thoughtful and careful consideration went into examining two structurally unsound beliefs which needed to be demolished. These beliefs were constructed in my early life with my parents who did not yet know God. These beliefs would no longer serve His temple being built in the Kingdom according to His Word. These were the feelings and beliefs that no longer served my new life in Christ:

1.) Feeling unworthy of healthy love, particularly from a man.

2.) Feeling ashamed and burdensome for having needs, values, and desires because for the majority of my early life, this was an area that had been neglected.

These non-supportive beams needed to be replaced by the Carpenter who does His reconstruction in the new life where He is lifted high in all areas.

He then laid it on my heart to have three new support beams (beliefs). The Lord nudged my heart with these truths:

1.) He reminded me of the new heart given by Him in Ezekial 34:17 is His treasure and not just a place for any man to access. This is why He said, "Above all else, guard your heart for out of it flow the issues of life." You are His treasured possession.

2.)   He said, "You are worthy of respect, worth the wait, and to be safely held in high regard as my beloved child."

3.)   He gently reminded me, "I am always, and again, I say always with you."

"And behold, I am with you always, to the end of the age" (Matthew 28:20 KJV).

"Behold" in the Greek translation according to the Strong's concordance means, "to attend to carefully, to guard, to keep, one in the state in which he is, to observe, to reserve, to undergo something." May we always remember He is not only with us now but within us for eternity. There is no closer, more intimate relationship we can have than with Jesus Christ, by the indwelling Holy Spirit.

After God revealed these three truths, I continued my visual journaling. I began drawing a water well made of bricks. Before I looked into the well where my deeper vulnerabilities are, I wrote the specifics of what a man of God, with His permission to access my heart, would reflect in his thoughts, words, and actions.

Each brick had qualities from the Word of God. Qualities that by faith in God are also true of myself. Some examples are: *"born again" of His Spirit* (paraphrased John 3:3 KJV) and bearing the *fruits of the Holy Ghost* (Read Galatians 5:22 KJV). These qualities are essential in being successfully matched in the royal family of God. In the season or lifetime of singleness, it is important to remember we are reflecting all these qualities back to God, who they are derived from.

Reflection Questions

What faulty beliefs do you need to replace in your heart and mind?

What biblical truths do you want to replace them with?

How has doing this activity impacted you?

God Restores

During this season, the Lord gave me a couple dreams. The first dream was of a multicolored robe that looked like someone had colored with markers. I didn't do the usual biblical research normally conducted when a dream is vivid and detailed. I basically brushed it aside. Then I had another similar dream with a colored robe. The story of Joesph initially came to mind, but rather the Lord led me to the story of the prodigal son. The most applicable verses are found in Luke 15:20-24 AMPC, where *"the Father clothed him in a robe and put a ring on him when he returned home. He got up and came to his [own] father. But while he was still a long way off, his father saw him and was moved with pity and tenderness [for him]; and he ran and embraced him and kissed him [fervently]."*

"And the son said to him, 'Father, I have sinned against heaven and in your sight; I am no longer worthy to be called your son [I no longer deserve to be recognized as a son of yours]!' But the father said to his bond servants, 'Bring quickly the best robe (the festive robe of honor) and put it on him; and give him a ring for his hand and sandals for his feet. And bring out that [wheat-]fattened calf and kill it; and

let us revel and feast and be happy and make merry, because this my son was dead and is alive again; he was lost and is found!' And they began to revel and feast and make merry."

I could relate to the prodigal son, needing to return to the Father's embrace and have Him clothe me with His best robe, His righteousness to cover my shame of sin, as a result of foolishly partaking of the world once again. The ring was another confirmation of what I believed the Lord wanted me to do next: to exchange my old jewelry and to buy a quaint pearl ring. This ring would be a reminder of a promise and commitment to first honor the Lord with my body, to make a commitment to Him of celibacy until the bridegroom He has for me makes me his bride.

The ring's pearl reminds me of His blood-bought purchase of me and how I was brought into His Kingdom and no longer belong to this world. It serves as a reminder that this flesh can no longer dominate, but His Spirit must forever reign supreme in my inner being. The pearl is significant of the parable found in Matthew 14:44-46 KJV.

"Again, the kingdom of heaven is like unto a merchant man, seeking goodly pearls: Who, when he had found one pearl of great price, went and sold all that he had, and bought it."

We are that pearl of great price! He gave His very life to redeem us from sin and shame that we may shine forth and glorify His holy name.

Reflection Questions

What do you need God to restore in your life?

How can you trust He is restoring while you wait on His promises to be fulfilled?

What are some actions you can take in the restoration process of replacing old beliefs with new reminders of what He has said according to His Word (faith and works)? (ex. I have a dear sister in Christ who bought a mug that says husband because she is believing God for one ordained by Him).

Obedience to His Leading

"For this God is our God for ever and ever: he will be our guide even unto death." Psalm 48:14 KJV

A dear sister in Christ boldly went on social media proclaiming some really difficult generational things she wanted broken in her family. She declared in the video recording that she had been running from the Lord and knew she needed to be brave and do as He was asking her. This boldness she shared, even with voice quaking, ignited me to also do the very same. I knew the Lord wanted me to continue writing this book. She was also being rewarded for her obedience in the reconciling of her family, which had formerly experienced much brokenness. This is a job that only the Lord God up above can so assuredly complete.

When we are public with our sins, issues, hurts, and requests, it is especially vulnerable. It is not just putting the matters in God's hands in private but also in the midst of witnesses, which include individuals with varying measures of faith, as well as the critics. Jesus also dealt with many critics everywhere He went.

Yet the Lord loves our faith. Without it we really do not have a relationship with God. So much of building trust with Him will stem first from having faith and then moving into action.

"And without faith it is impossible to please Him, for whoever would draw near to God must believe that He exists and that He rewards those who diligently seek Him." Hebrews 11:36 KJV

Living a Life of Biblical Value

Something I had been so honored to experience was going on a Scripture memorizing retreat. With about twenty-five other followers of Christ, we memorized together. I was especially determined to attend the retreat because the previous years involved the birth of my niece, recovering from a painful hip injury, and attempting to busy myself and run from the grief.

This year I could not miss the opportunity. Instead of my annual trip outside of Wisconsin with a dear sister in Christ, I was able to invite her to the Northern woods. This would be an experience she would cherish for the remainder of her life on this earth, however, never knew it would be as impactful as it was.

There is such a beauty, a purity, a wholesomeness that comes with being with other followers of Christ in a sole focus on planting the Word deep in our hearts. In this dedicated time and place, we would worship, recite, and help one another along in these eternal truths. We would pray, encourage one another, and learn of all the varying things the Lord was doing in each one of our lives while keeping Him at the forefront of our conversation and collective minds. It was such an enriching time in God's beautiful creation.

Memorized Verses –
Being on the Same Page

It is interesting to note how I came to know of this memorizing retreat. Years ago, a beautiful older couple I knew ended up purchasing the home I was renting. Their family and my roommate's family had been well acquainted for decades. The husband had invited me to a Scripture memorizing retreat. He explained families came up there all together for a weekend and took to memorizing passages of Scripture to song and also creating skits/plays. It was such a blessing to go and experience this spiritually edifying time away.

Following that experience, perhaps a year later, the two of them were at home in the kitchen. They began reciting Romans 8 together, helping one another along, smiling, spurring one another along so lovingly. It was such a moment of awe and wonder for me, as I realized this was exactly what a covenant marriage is to look like. We are so lovingly meant to reflect the Word of God one to another, not just in a manner of speaking but in deed, also. After witnessing this encounter, a very strong desire was planted within for a future relationship to be on the same page, and a biblical one at that.

Qualifiers

Healthy Attachment: Christ and the Father

"And in the morning, rising up a great while before day, he went out, and departed into a solitary place, and there prayed." Mark 1:35 KJV

As I began taking time to study healthy relational attachment styles, it became more and more apparent that Christ modeled a secure attachment with the Father. In order to rewire my own early programming, I needed to truly understand and witness what healthy attachment looked like. Jesus began His day on the earth in prayer, particularly when His ministry began. When we value a relationship, this relationship becomes our number one priority. We want to spend time with this individual, not just any haphazard time, but quality time. Memorable time.

Since the Lord is our husband, our first love, He desires to woo us and continually remind us of His limitless love in the face of grief, sorrow, and hurts that come in this life. Until we realize He is the source of our every healing, in whatever way He orchestrates it, we will continue to try to fix, heal, and facilitate a corrective experience and may be tempted to go outside of His will in an attempt to place a Band-Aid on a wound that only He can bandage and breathe life back into.

Spending quality time in the Word and in prayer, trusting fully that if there is a Word on it, it will come to pass, fills me up spiritually for the start of the day. It gives me sustenance to draw from throughout the day. I also like to take time to nibble and snack on spiritual food throughout the day. We have so many options online, but I also want to warn you to please be careful that what we are listening to aligns with the Bible and not a human being twisting it to tickle our ears or appeal to our carnal (or surface level) desires.

Reflection Questions

How will you prioritize your time with Him?

How will you be mindful to see the evidence of His faithful love?

Confirmations

Obedience and humility are key in living a life pleasing to God. The question is how can we keep these concepts at the forefront of our minds, especially when they are so countercultural. Sometimes it will feel like in your obedience you are losing, and you may very well be losing, but rejoice because who or what you are losing isn't what God intends for you keep. This is why feelings can be misleading. How can it feel like you're losing but in obedience you are really winning? When discouragement sets in, it is important to do a biblical study regarding the rewards of obedience to increase your faith and trump your momentary feelings.

The Word of God says, "even *though Jesus was God's Son he learned obedience from the things He suffered..."* (Hebrews 5:8 NLT). This was speaking of when He was about to be crucified and prayed a desperate prayer to be spared, yet surrendered His flesh to the will of the Father.

Praying in the mighty name of Jesus when suffering and trials come, we remember Your willing sacrifice and know whatever is currently being experienced is nothing in comparison to that. May we fix our eyes on all You overcame, knowing we have the same power that was in You that overcame the grave. Thank You, Jesus, for every victory we have be granted in You! May we have a new pattern of overcoming every enticement of the flesh, every snare the enemy sets, and every previous generational cycle! May we overcome by the blood of the Lamb and the word of our testimony. In Jesus name, amen.

Reminder

*"Every believer is ultimately responsible for his or her own conscious."*Galatians 6:4-5 TPT

Even God's very best man or woman for you is still just a man or a woman, subject to the very same fleshly temptations as you. The only confidence we can have is in Christ, not in any flesh, not ours or others. Our flesh must be crucified daily, or it is too often attempting to get in the way. My best friend recently reminded me to pray in my prayer language, particularly when emotions start to rise. The enemy first entered the picture in between a man and a woman, to drive a wedge between them and God. He is still using the very same tactic. This is why it is important for you both to know the areas you need fortified faith to close any entry point to the enemy.

May we keep God first in all we say, think, and do. May His love continually take first place in our lives. May His love be the source of our every motivation. May we keep His truth where it can be easily drawn from at all times, in our hearts and at the forefront of our minds. May we draw from the well of living waters. May His goodness ever be enough, even when our emotions want us to believe otherwise and agree with any lies of the enemy. May we stand firm in the truth that so graciously sets us free. Not our truth but His, which is not only pertinent to this life on earth but for the heaven we can experience here and now when we surrender our will for His day by day!

Also remember, if you are still feeling shame over the past after seeking forgiveness from Christ, the Word of God promises us, *"For your shame ye shall have double; everlasting joy shall be unto them"* (paraphrased Isaiah 61:7). So go ahead and trade that shame for faith in double, shame in exchange for abounding joy because of who He is and all He has done on your behalf.

If you are still experiencing any emotional weight, meditate and chew on this eternal exchange in which no other exchange can compare. There is no better exchange system you can find on earth. He has already exchanged our sins for entrance into what is eternal—heaven.

"To give them beauty for ashes, the oil of joy for mourning, the garment of praise for the spirit of heaviness; that they might be called trees of righteousness, the planting of the Lord, that He might be glorified." Isaiah 61:2-3 KJV

Cling fast to His Word if you need more faith, it is yours for the asking. *"You have not because you ask not"* (James 4:2 KJV). We ask according to the will of God. Sometimes it can be the simplest of things we neglect to ask for. Ask, believe, and receive with a heart of great gratitude unto the God, *"who is able to do exceedingly beyond all we can ask or hope by the power He has invested within us"*(Ephesians 3:20 KJV).

Preparing For the Wedding Supper of the Lamb

"Then I heard what seemed to be the voice of the great multitude like the roar of many waters and the sound of mighty peals of thunder, crying out,

'Hallelujah! For the Lord our God the Almighty reigns. Let us rejoice and exult and give Him glory, for the marriage of the Lamb has come, and His bride has made herself ready; it was granted her to clothe herself with fine linen, bright and pure' For the fine linen is the righteous deeds of the saints. And the angel said to me, 'Write this, "Blessed are those who are invited to the marriage supper of the Lamb."' And he said to me, 'These are the true words of God."

Revelation 19:6-9 ESV

Recognizing God is my faithful husband who will never change, never fail, and continues to love me in spite of my unsteadiness humbles me greatly. How I long for Him to rescue me from this struggle with the flesh and to ever be the conqueror His Word declares that we are. When envisioning the wedding supper of the Lamb, it is going to be a glorious occasion. We can think of the world's very best presentation times ten or one hundred. Unlike living in this fallen world, we will ever be entering into His perfection.

There will be no more temptations, no more struggling. No more worries needing to be reframed with faith. No more heartaches, for His love will ever take first place. His love will remain supreme. No more evil to contend with. No more grief, no more loss, no more questions to be asked. Just a beautiful harmony as it was originally intended with no sin, lie, or evil coming in between us and the Heavenly Father. All because of the incredible sacrifice paid on our behalf by Jesus Christ, God's very own Son and our belief that He is the truth, the life, and the way!

"And I fell at his feet to worship him. And he said unto me, 'See thou do it not: I am thy fellowservant, and of thy brethren that have the testimony of Jesus: worship God: for the testimony of Jesus is the spirit of prophecy.'

And I saw heaven opened, and behold a white horse; and he that sat upon him was called Faithful and True, and in righteousness he doth judge and make war.

His eyes were as a flame of fire, and on his head were
many crowns; and he had a name written, that no man
knew, but he himself.

And he was clothed with a vesture dipped in blood: and his
name is called The Word of God.

And the armies which were in heaven followed him upon
white horses, clothed in fine linen, white and clean.

And out of his mouth goeth a sharp sword, that with it he
should smite the nations: and he shall rule them with a rod
of iron: and he treadeth the winepress of the fierceness and
wrath of Almighty God.

And he hath on his vesture and on his thigh a name written,
KING OF KINGS, AND LORD OF LORDS.

And I saw an angel standing in the sun; and he cried with a
loud voice, saying to all the fowls that fly in the midst of
heaven, 'Come and gather yourselves together unto the
supper of the great God;

That ye may eat the flesh of kings, and the flesh of captains,
and the flesh of mighty men, and the flesh of horses, and of

them that sit on them, and the flesh of all men, both free

and bond, both small and great.'"

Revelation 19:10-18 KJV

Now when I ended reading here, I thought to myself, this is not quite what I imagined. Then I remembered God is not playing with evil, and this is why we need to examine ourselves to make sure there is nothing evil operating in us. He is a holy and righteous God, and He requires we also be holy and set apart for His purposes.

These biblical realities can put the fear of God back into our hearts. As Ray Comfort states, in these instances, "fear is our friend, when it is saving our life," and in this instance to life eternal.

God is Looking for a Pure and Spotless Bride

"And he opened his mouth, and taught them, saying,
'Blessed are the poor in spirit:
for theirs is the kingdom of heaven.
Blessed are they that mourn: for they shall be comforted.
Blessed are the meek: for they shall inherit the earth.
Blessed are they which do hunger and thirst after
righteousness: for they shall be filled.
Blessed are the merciful: for they shall obtain mercy.
Blessed are the pure in heart: for they shall see
God.'"

Matthew 5:2-8 KJV

God is looking for purity. He is preparing us for the life to come. Purity isn't just about abstaining from sexual immorality but everything we think, say, and do, whatever we are taking in, looking at, and consuming.

Prayer for God to have first place in every area of our lives, molding and shaping us, cleaning and refreshing us. He was a carpenter for a reason. Building and finishing His creation to reflect His glory! May we all remain humbly fortified in all that He has already placed inside us.

"The daughters of kings, women of honor,
are maidens in your courts.
And standing beside you,
glistening in your pure and golden glory,
is the beautiful bride-to-be!
Now listen, daughter, pay attention,
and forget about your past.
Put behind you every attachment to the familiar,
even those who once were close to you!
For your royal Bridegroom is ravished by your
beautiful brightness.
Bow in reverence before him, for he is your Lord!"

Psalm 45:9-11 TPT

..."But When the Desire Cometh It is a Tree of Life"

Proverbs 13:12 KJV

Answered Prayers while finalizing this book...

While this book was in the final stages of completion, God so lovingly restored the relationship between my mother and I. Shortly afterwards she gave her life to Christ which was a prayer prayed for 35 years.

He also restored the relationship with my oldest daughter and I. She too is saved and walking with Christ for the last 3 years. She is also now married to a Christian man and he too is an answer to 1,000 prayers as he loves the Lord and wants to continue leading my daughter in her prioritizing God and serving His kingdom.

This is further evidence of His faithfulness and I pray it encourages you in any relationships you are trusting Him to restore. *"God is not a respecter of a person,"* meaning what He has done for one, He will do for another. He has no favorites but the closer we draw near to Him, the closer He draws near to us.

Stay encouraged!

Acknowledgements

First and foremost all thanks and praise be to God, my Abba, for His FAITHFULNESS. He has been my Help, the Lifter of my heart, the Wind in my sails to keep me going time and time again. Where would I be without Him? I shudder to even imagine. Am eternally grateful for the Endless Gift that He is and ever will be to each and every one of us who puts our hope and trust in Him. Jesus, Prince of Peace, the One who stills the storms and the ones He allows, promises the Holy Spirit to be our God of all comfort, our counselor and so much more. Thank You to the Three in One God who moves mountains and whom death could not hold. Praying and trusting You All will keep me as I go forth in the plan and calling.

This book would not be possible without the many who has cheered me on courageously in faith. My Mothers in the faith: Adrienne Kuehl, who was my first spiritual mother, from the age of seventeen. Thank you for being a beacon of grace and evangelism. Veronica Ventrice, who faithfully discipled me for years showing me how to live out the Word of God. Pastor Catherine Richards who declared exactly who God had created me to be. Mother Joycelyn Henderson who declared I was a writer from our first introduction and modeled the most excellent way. Mother Washington, who is now in the Great Cloud of Witness, who fanned the flame and stirred the gifts every time I was able to be in her presence. She would say, "God has placed many books inside of you," as she lovingly placed her hand on my belly. To my beloved Pastor, who is a man who models seeking to please God is all His ways. Thank you for being my example of a godly man. To Britt Van Asbach, a dear sister, who has encouraged me time and time again, "write that down, put that in the book," and the one who would be there in any needful time, thank you. In times of grief, especially, I need you as God has gifted you to care in the most crucial of times.

To Steven & Sandy Walker who bring the Word to life in fun and creative ways as a means to disciple many. Beth Kettner who I met shortly after the loss of Kobe, who taught me the greater importance of more securely attaching myself to Christ in greater surrender. Wanda Boggs for proofreading, providing necessary feedback, encouraging and offering to pray any time. Patricia Winfrey, who came alongside just at the right time, encouraging me to crucify the flesh and finish the book.

There are many others whom I cannot express enough thanks for including my parents and family, as well as those who cared for me through the years, lovingly taking me under their wings. I stand in confident expectation His Perfect Love has already won regarding each of you, your children and children's children.

To Ella and Emma, may you girls be free to be everything God created you to be.

Thank you Sister Daphynie for bringing conviction in our first time having one on one fellowship to be obedient to the call. Thank you Sister Ladonna for being willing to find my mom so her and I could reunite.

To the men in the story. Thank you for the season in which we shared and to my ex-husband, for our beautiful daughters. Like a book, we carry the chapters with us and I am so grateful for the positive memories, the painful times and the lessons learned. Most of all that each one helped me realize it was Christ I needed more of all along....